CW00410442

Getting started with

THEORY

beginner to grade 2

by Nicholas Keyworth

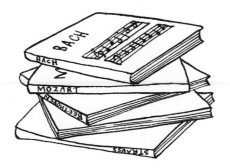

TRINITY · FABER

Faber Music 3 Queen Square London WC1N 3AU

in association with

Trinity College *London* 89 Albert Embankment London SE1 7TP

Foreword

Music theory is often neglected due to lack of time in instrumental lessons. However, an understanding of theory helps everyone to play from music accurately, learn pieces more quickly, play music with other people, write music down and perhaps achieve better marks in exams!

This book is a simple introduction to music theory which develops skills in a gradual and fun way. Written to help teachers incorporate theory into lessons, with a great range of activities for pupils to take home and complete as part of practice time, the integrated approach means theory can become an integral part of every instrumental lesson.

Getting started with theory is a players' guide which looks at the practical aspects of theory, covering subjects up to Grade 2 of the Trinity syllabus. Those intending to take a theory exam should refer to the Trinity *Theory Workbooks* and Trinity syllabus.

Answers for all the numbered questions in the book are available on the *Getting started* website: www.fabermusic.com/gettingstarted

© 2003 by Faber Music Ltd and Trinity College *London*
First published in 2003 by Faber Music Ltd
in association with Trinity College *London*
3 Queen Square London WC1N 3AU
Cover illustration by Jan McCafferty
Music processed by Stave Origination
Printed in England by Caligraving Ltd
All rights reserved

ISBN 0–571–52195–1

To buy Faber Music or Trinity publications or to find out about the full range of titles available please contact your local music retailer or Faber Music sales enquiries:

Faber Music Ltd, Burnt Mill, Elizabeth Way, Harlow CM20 2HX
Tel: +44 (0)1279 82 89 82   Fax: +44 (0)1279 82 89 83
sales@fabermusic.com   fabermusic.com   trinitycollege.co.uk

Getting started

The easiest way to write down music is through graphic notation, using shapes and symbols to represent the sounds.

What sort of a sound do you think the shape below represents? Try playing or singing it:

Now think about these questions on what you have just played:

☐ What *notes* did you play/sing?

☐ How *long* were the notes?

☐ How *loud* or *soft* were the notes?

☐ How *fast* or *slow* was it?

☐ Were there any *silences* between the sounds?

☐ Were the sounds *smooth* or *detached*?

Play or sing the shape again now you have thought about these questions. Did you play it quite differently?

Here is the same idea written on a stave. Try playing it:

Because more information is given here it is possible to play it more accurately.

Using graphic notation

Think of the first phrase of a piece you know well. Without looking at the music, draw a shape to represent it in the box below. Check the list above and include as many of those elements as possible in your shape.

Have a go at drawing your own graphic notation in Getting started with *composition.*

Piece title: ....

High and low

Musical notes are written on a stave, which shows us how **high** or **low** the notes are. Notes are named in the order of the first seven letters of the alphabet, A to G. The clef at the start tells us which set of letters to use – a treble clef for higher notes and a bass clef for lower ones.

The treble clef is also known as the G clef because it starts on the second line up, where the note G is.

Treble clef notes

① Write the letter names below these notes, starting with D. After the note G start again with the letter A.

Complete a line of treble clefs starting on the second line up:

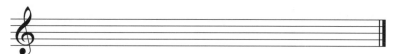

Try not to lift your pencil off the paper until each one is complete

② Write down the names of these treble clef notes:

Bass clef notes

③ Fill in the letter names below these notes, starting with F.

Complete a line of bass clefs starting on the second line down. Don't forget the dots!

The bass clef is also known as the F clef because it starts on the second line down, where the note F is.

④ Write down the names of these bass clef notes:

Which clef an instrument uses usually depends on whether it is high or low in pitch. An alto clef is used for just one or two instruments, and is pitched between treble and bass clefs.

Which clef does your instrument use? _____

⑤ Find out which clefs these instruments use:

Flute _____

Bassoon _____

Piano _____

Viola _____

Trumpet _____

Leger lines

If we need to write notes higher or lower than the stave we need to add little extra lines called leger lines.

Always check the clef before working out the notes

Here are some notes on leger lines. Working up or down from the last note you know, work out the name of each:

⑦ Write a treble or bass clef before each note to make the letter name correct:

A   F   G   C   C   D   F   D   C

Note Connections

⑧ Draw a line to connect each note to its correct note name:

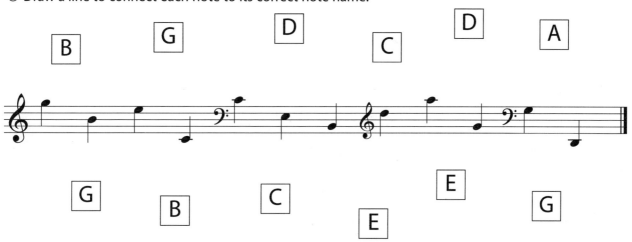

Long and short

Imagine each of these lines is a note. Choose one pitch and try playing or singing them. Don't forget the gaps as well.

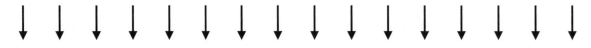

We need more information than this to know how long notes should be. The first thing to do is keep a steady beat or pulse as we play: rather like a metronome or clock ticking away at the same pace.

Here the pulse is shown by the arrows above the notes. Set your metronome to ♩ = 60 and play or sing it against this steady pulse:

Now we need an easier way of showing the length of notes than drawing lines.

Note lengths

A one beat note is called a **crotchet** (or 'quarter note'):

Draw 8 crotchets on this line. Choose a pitch and play them with a steady pulse (one on each beat).

A two beat note is called a **minim** (or 'half note'):

Draw 4 minims on this line. Choose a pitch and play them with a steady pulse (count two beats for each note):

Now try mixing them up! On the line below write down a mixture of crotchets and minims. Then choose a pitch and play or sing them with a steady beat:

Instead of tapping your foot count 'one, two' in your head with each note.

There are several more note lengths you will come across. We also need to show the lengths of silences between the notes, which are called **rests**. Here is a table showing notes and rests, their names and values:

Name	Duration	Note	Rest
Semibreve (or whole note)	4 beats	𝅝	▬
Minim (or half note)	2 beats	𝅗𝅥	▬
Crotchet (or quarter note)	1 beat	♩	𝄽
Quaver (or eighth note)	½ beat	♪	𝄾
Semiquaver (or sixteenth note)	¼ beat	𝅘𝅥𝅯	𝄿
Demisemiquaver (or thirty-second note)	⅛ beat	𝅘𝅥𝅰	𝅀

Pick three different note lengths then improvise a series of notes of each value on one or two pitches only. Call the piece The clock shop. *The semibreve could be a grandfather clock, the semiquaver a small alarm clock, and so on.*

Beams

Did you notice that the shorter notes have tails as well as stems? If you use two or more of these notes together, instead of writing tails, join them together with a beam like this:

Add up how many crotchet beats the following groups of notes and rests make:

⑨

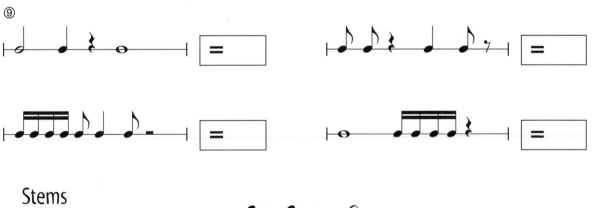

Stems

Most notes have stems like this: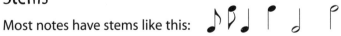

Usually, any note written **on or above** the middle line on a stave should have its stem going **down**. Any note written **below** the middle line should have its stem going **up**.

Which note value does not have a stem?

⑩ Draw the correct stems on these crotchet notes (the first two have been done already):

Sometimes we have to change the rule of stems going up or down because we are using beams. Here is an example:

⑪ On the stave below, draw in the correct notes and note lengths. Make sure notes are joined by a beam if necessary, and that your stems go the correct way:

Choose notes within the stave

Crotchet D   Semiquaver B, C, D, E   Quavers G, A

Two quaver Es   Minim C   Semibreve F (lower)

Dots

If we add a dot after a note like this it makes the note **half as long again**.

⑫ Draw the following notes and work out how many crotchet beats these notes would be worth:

Dotted crotchet   ♩.   = 1½ beats

Dotted semibreve   ___   _____

Dotted minim   ___   _____

Dotted quaver   ___   _____

How many crotchet beats do each of these add up to:

⑬

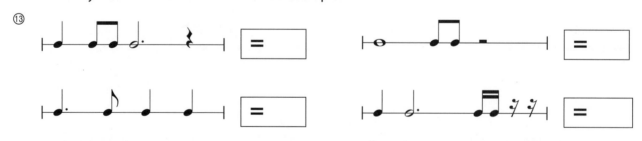

⑭ On the line below draw in the correct notes:

Crotchet   Four semiquavers   Crotchet rest   Dotted crotchet

Crotchet   Crotchet   Pair of quavers   Quaver

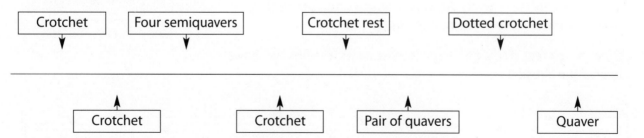

Clap this rhythm and then play it on one or two notes on your instrument.

Grouping notes

Time signatures

A time signature is the two numbers at the start of a piece. It tells us how many beats there are in each bar and the value of each of these beats.

The top number tells us **how many** beats there are in each bar:

Top number	Number of beats in each bar
2	2 beats in a bar
3	3 beats in a bar
4	4 beats in a bar
5	5 beats in a bar

Barlines divide music into small groups of notes called bars.

The bottom number is a code which tells us **the value** of each beat:

Bottom number	Value of each beat
2	Minim
4	Crotchet
8	Quaver

A semibreve rest is also a whole bar rest in any time signature.

So if we have a time signature of $\frac{3}{4}$ it means there are 3 crotchet beats in each bar.

⑮ Explain the following time signatures (the first one has been done for you):

Time signature	Explanation
$\frac{2}{4}$	2 crotchet beats in a bar.
$\frac{3}{8}$	
$\frac{4}{4}$	
$\frac{2}{2}$	
$\frac{5}{4}$	
$\frac{4}{2}$	

Can you improvise a phrase in $\frac{2}{4}$ and $\frac{3}{4}$? How different do they feel?

The notes and rests in each bar of a piece of music should add up to the number of beats given in the time signature. So with a time signature of $\frac{3}{4}$ each bar should add up to 3 crotchet beats.

Barlines

For each of the following passages, look at the time signature then draw in the barlines:

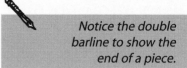

Notice the double barline to show the end of a piece.

Ties

Ties join two or more notes together to make a single longer note. A tie is often used to hold a note over a barline. Can you find any ties in your own pieces? How many crotchet beats should these tied notes be held for:

Grouping notes

Notes are grouped into beats whenever possible. This makes it easier to read music. Here are some different ways that quavers and semiquavers can be grouped:

Quavers and semiquavers are grouped together by beams.

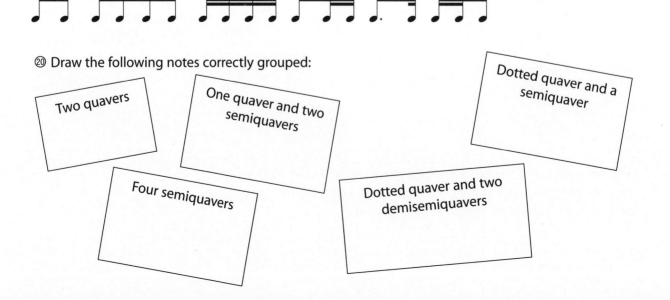

⑳ Draw the following notes correctly grouped:

Two quavers

One quaver and two semiquavers

Dotted quaver and a semiquaver

Four semiquavers

Dotted quaver and two demisemiquavers

Up-beats

When music doesn't start on the first beat of a bar this is called an anacrusis or up-beat. The first and final bars need to add up to one complete bar in value.

Do any of your pieces start on an up-beat? What does it feel like when an up-beat starts a piece?

Fill in the remaining barlines in the following pieces:

㉑

㉒

Write the correct time signature at the beginning of each of these bars:

㉓

Triplets

Sometimes three notes are played in the time of two; this is called a **triplet**.
As well as writing the three notes, we need to group them together with a '3'
like this:

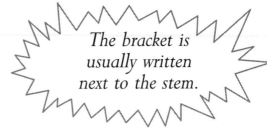

The bracket is usually written next to the stem.

㉔ Copy the following passage, replacing all the pairs of quavers with triplets.

Keys and key signatures

Sharps, flats and naturals

To understand sharps, flats and naturals it's easiest to look at the piano keyboard. This shows all the notes, laid out in order. The black notes are the sharp and flat notes, either side of the white notes.

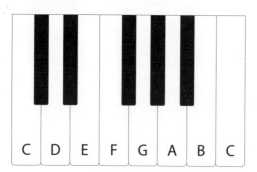

Sharps, flats and naturals are also known as accidentals.

If we were to play all these notes (black and white) in order, we would have a **chromatic scale**, where all the notes are next door to one another. Next door notes are a **semitone** apart. How many notes would there be in a chromatic scale if you played it on the keyboard above?

_____

The white notes are the **natural** notes. The box below shows a natural sign. Complete a line of natural signs next to it:

♮

A natural sign is used to cancel a sharp or flat

The black key one semitone higher (to the right) of a white note is the **sharp** of that white note. A sharp sign is shown below. Complete a line of sharps next to it:

♯

The black key one semitone lower (to the left) of a white note is a **flat**. The box below shows a flat sign. Complete a line of flats next to it:

♭

Two **semitones** equal one **tone**, for example G to A, or E to F sharp.

㉕ Using the keyboard diagram above, work out the following notes:

What note is a tone above D?   _____

What note is a tone above B?   _____

What note is a tone above F♯?   _____

What note is a tone below E♭?   _____

What note is a tone below C?   _____

Remember sharper is higher, flatter is lower.

㉖ Write down the names of these notes:

—   —   —   —   —   —   —   —   —

Major scales

Scales follow a set pattern of semitones and tones. Major scales follow this pattern:

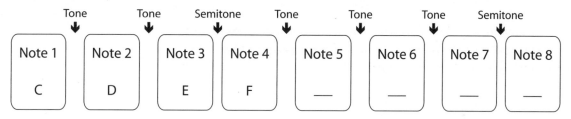

So in a scale of C major, note one would be C, the next a tone above would be D, another tone E, then a semitone F – and so on. In the boxes above complete the note names for C major.

㉗ Using the pattern of tones and semitones given above, write down the notes you would play in the scale of G major. Don't forget any sharps or flats!

| G | | | | | | | |

Use the keyboard on p.12 to help you. Try playing these on your instrument.

㉘ Do the same for the scale of A major:

| A | | | | | | | |

㉙ Write down the notes you would play in the scale of F major:

| F | | | | | | | |

㉚ On the stave below, write an ascending scale of A major. Don't forget a clef for your instrument and any sharps or flats:

Ascending = going up
Descending = going down

㉛ Here is a melody in A major. Add sharps or flats to any notes which need them to make this melody correct. A sharp or flat added to a note will affect it for the rest of that bar. Now play or sing it: does it sound right?

Key signatures

Pieces of music are usually based around the notes of a scale. This is known as the **key** of that piece. That means some notes in the piece are always sharp or flat. To save writing a sharp or flat sign every time these notes are played, we write a **key signature** at the start of each line of music.

㉜ How many sharps were there in G major (p.13)? ☐

How many sharps were there in A major (p.13)? ☐

How many flats were there in F major (p.13)? ☐

㉝ Name the sharps or flats in the following keys. Work out the scales first using the pattern given on p.13. Then work out how many sharps and flats are needed. Play each scale to check it sounds right.

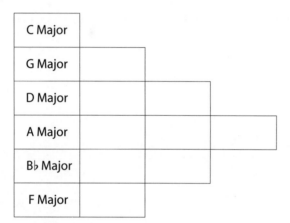

C Major has no sharps or flats in its key signature.

Are any of your pieces in these keys? Check the key signatures.

Minor keys

Each major key shares its key signature with a minor key. This links them so they are known as each other's relative major or minor.

☐ To find the relative minor of a major key you need to find the **sixth note** of the scale. If you are in C major the sixth note is A: so the relative minor of C major is A minor.

☐ To find the relative major of a minor key you need to find the **third note** of the scale. If you are in A minor the third note is C – so its relative major is C major.

㉞ What is the relative minor of the following major keys:

C Major	G Major	D Major	A Major	B♭ Major	F Major
A Minor					

Minor scales

There are two main types of minor scale: **harmonic** and **melodic**. On this page we will just look at harmonic. Harmonic minor scales have the same key signature as their relative major, but use different patterns of tones and semitones to major scales:

❑ The third note is a **semitone lower** than in major scales.

❑ The seventh note is **raised a semitone**. This is not included in the key signature so needs to be added as an accidental.

So, A harmonic minor has the same key signature as C major, a flattened third (C♮) and the seventh note is raised to G♯.

> *Remember!*
> *Ascending = going up*
> *Descending = going down*

㉟ Write a clef for your instrument, any key signature needed and the scale of **A harmonic minor** ascending, with any sharps or flats required.

Relative major of A minor: _____   Key signature: _____

㊱ Now do the same for the scale of **D harmonic minor** ascending. Don't forget the key signature and clef!

Relative major of D minor: _____   Key signature: _____

㊲ Write out the scale of **B harmonic minor** descending, with the key signature and any accidentals needed.

Play each scale after you have written it. Can you recognise the sound of a minor scale?

Try to find two pieces you know in minor keys. Write down their titles then see if you can answer the following questions about them.

Title: _____   Key: _____

Relative major: _____   Accidentals: _____

Title: _____   Key: _____

Relative major: _____   Accidentals: _____

Intervals

Tones and semitones are one way of measuring the distance between notes. Another system names the notes rather like a staircase.

Here is a scale of 8 notes:

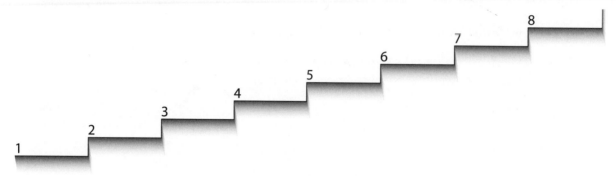

Next to each number write the letter names of a scale of C major ascending. The interval from note one to note two is a **second**. In fact it is a **major second** because this is a major scale. From note one to five is a **fifth** and so on. We can do this in any key – as long as we think of the first note as note number one of the scale.

Major intervals

Intervals of a 2nd, 3rd, 6th and 7th are all major intervals if the notes are part of the major scale. Can you name the second note of these intervals if the first note is C?

㊳ Major 6th above C is _____   Major 2nd above C is _____

   Major 7th above C is _____   Major 3rd above C is _____

Now work out the second note of the interval if the first note is G:

㊴ Major 2nd above G is _____   Major 3rd above G is _____

   Major 6th above G is _____   Major 7th above G is _____

The first note in each of the following is different but the same rule applies – always count up from the first note to find the interval.

㊵ From D to F♯ is a _____   From B♭ to G is a _____

   From A to G♯ is a _____   From F to E is a _____

   From A to C♯ is a _____   From B♭ to C is a _____

   From F to G is a _____   From D to C♯ is a _____

Try to find an example of all of these intervals (2nd, 3rd, 6th and 7th) in pieces you know.

Minor intervals

If we lower major intervals of a 2nd, 3rd, 6th or 7th by a semitone they become **minor** intervals. So, if a major third is C to E, a **minor** third is C to E♭.

Work out the second note of the following minor intervals if the first note is G:

㊶ Minor 6th above G is _____

Minor 2nd above G is _____

Minor 7th above G is _____

Minor 3rd above G is _____

Name the intervals formed by the following notes:

㊷ From D to F is a _____   From C to A♭ is a _____

From A to C is a _____   From G to E♭ is a _____

From B to A is a _____   From E to F is a _____

From F to G♭ is a _____   From D to C is a _____

You may find it easier to work out the major interval first then lower it by a semitone.

Perfect intervals

Intervals of a 4th, 5th or 8ve (octave) are perfect intervals. These intervals remain the same whether in a major or minor key. The two notes of an octave interval (8 notes) have the same note name. Name the intervals formed by the following notes:

㊸ C to G is a _____

C to F is a _____

G to D is a _____

B♭ to E♭ is a _____

F to high F is an _____

Do you have a favourite interval? Pick one and improvise a short piece around it.

Mix it up

Now we've mixed up major, minor and perfect intervals. See if you can work them out. The first one has been done for you:

㊹ A to E is a perfect 5th   A to F♯ is a _____

D to F is a _____   F to F above is an _____

E to F♯ is a _____   E to G is a _____

D to B♭ is a _____   C to B♭ is a _____

F to B♭ is a _____   B to D♯ is a _____

Transposition

If we play music higher or lower than it was originally, we have **transposed** it. Continue to transpose this extract so you can play it an **octave** (8 notes) **higher**.

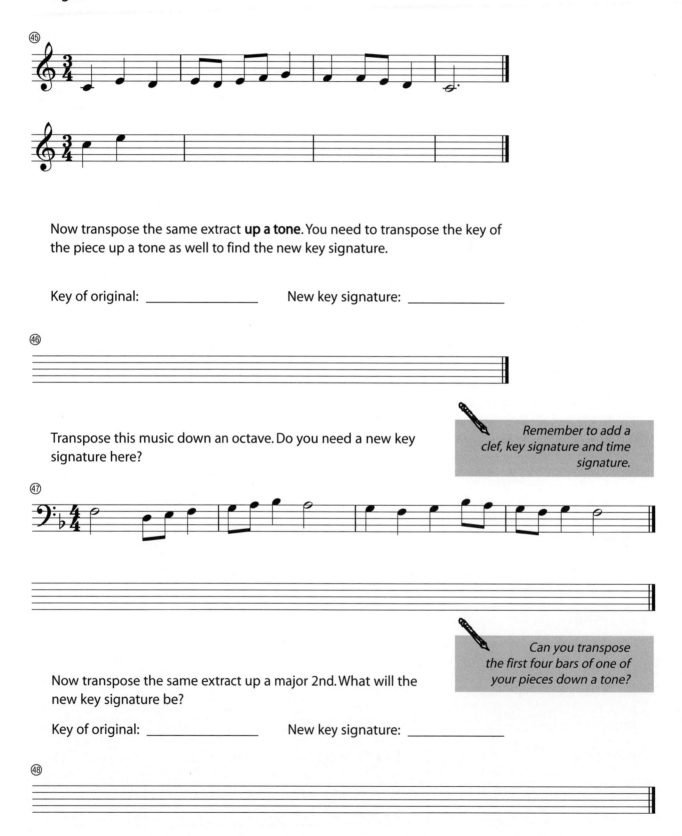

Now transpose the same extract **up a tone**. You need to transpose the key of the piece up a tone as well to find the new key signature.

Key of original: _____   New key signature: _____

Transpose this music down an octave. Do you need a new key signature here?

Remember to add a clef, key signature and time signature.

Now transpose the same extract up a major 2nd. What will the new key signature be?

Can you transpose the first four bars of one of your pieces down a tone?

Key of original: _____   New key signature: _____

Triads

When more than one note is played at the same time it is known
as a chord. A chord containing three notes is known as a triad. If
we play the first (tonic), third and fifth notes of a scale together,
we make a tonic triad:

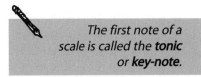

*The first note of a
scale is called the **tonic**
or **key-note**.*

④⑨ Write tonic triads for the following keys, then name the notes under each
chord (do not forget to add any sharps or flats).

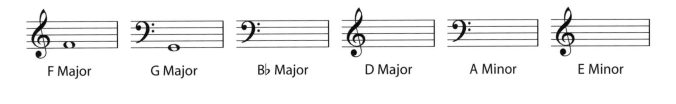

| F Major | G Major | B♭ Major | D Major | A Minor | E Minor |

_____   _____   _____   _____   _____   _____

Inversions

Here is a triad of C major written in three different ways. When the
tonic is at the bottom the triad is in **root position**:

If we re-arrange the notes like this, with the middle note (the 3rd)
at the bottom, it is called a **first inversion**:

With the top note of the triad (the 5th) at the bottom, it is called a
second inversion:

Chord connections

⑤⓪ Can you connect the correct name to each chord?

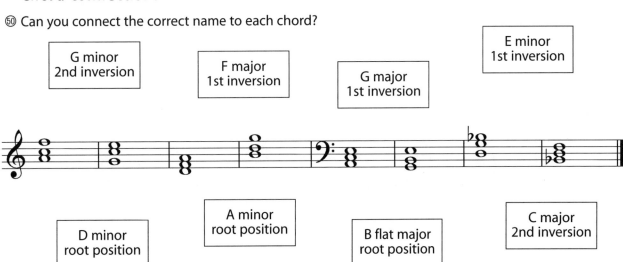

More triads

You can also build triads on other notes of the scale, not just the tonic. The two most important are built on the fourth and fifth notes of the scale:

> A chord built on the fourth note of the scale is called the **sub-dominant** (or chord IV).
>
> A chord built on the fifth note of the scale is called the **dominant** (or chord V).

Keyboard players can explore chords further in Getting started with keyboard musicianship.

The note on which any of these chords is built is known as the **root**.

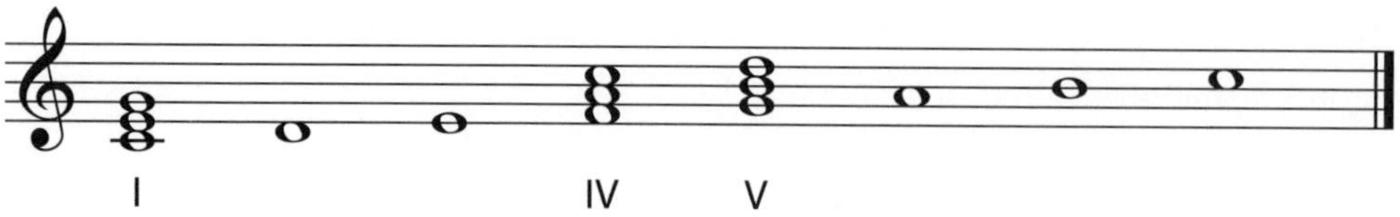
I
IV
V

Here are the scales of F and G major. Add the tonic, sub-dominant and dominant chords above the correct notes in each scale. Don't forget any accidentals necessary.

(51)

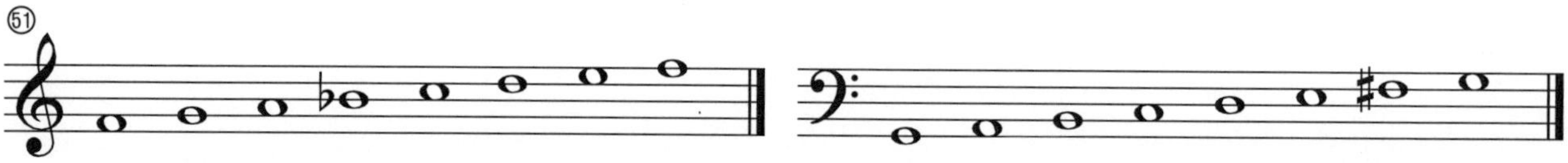

(52) Can you write the following triads?

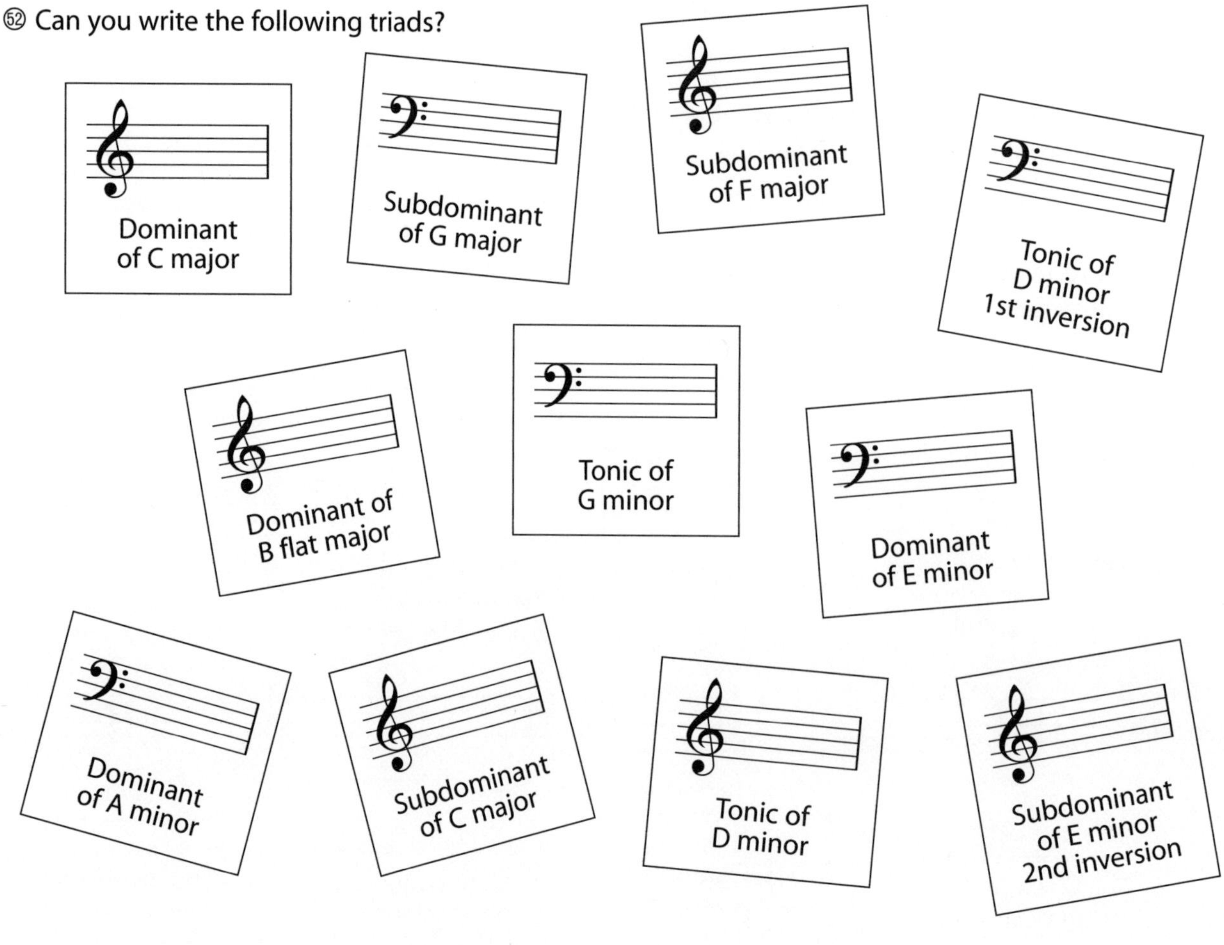
Dominant of C major
Subdominant of G major
Subdominant of F major
Tonic of D minor 1st inversion
Dominant of B flat major
Tonic of G minor
Dominant of E minor
Dominant of A minor
Subdominant of C major
Tonic of D minor
Subdominant of E minor 2nd inversion

Signs and symbols

In music, there are lots of signs telling you what to play and how to play it.

A **double barline** tells you you have reached
the end of the piece or the end of a section:

Two dots before a double barline means a
repeat. It tells you to go back to the beginning
or to the last set of dots and play that section again.

*Notice that the
second line is thicker
than the first.*

Sometimes, the composer might want you to repeat a section but end it
differently. Then you will see a **1st time** bar showing what you play the first
time through, and a **2nd time bar** for the second time through:

If you see the words **Da capo** (or **D.C.**) it means go back to the beginning
and play it through again. If you see the words **Dal segno** (or **D.S.**) it means
go back to the sign 𝄋 and play again. **Da capo al Fine** or **Dal segno al Fine**
both mean go back and play through again as far as the Fine sign.

A pause 𝄐 over a note means hold on to this note for longer than normal.

Look through some of the music you are learning at the moment. If you can
find any of the following, tick the box and fill in the title of the piece:

Sign	Tick	Title of Piece
Double barline		
Repeat sign		
1st time bar		
2nd time bar		
Da capo		
Dal segno		
Pause		

Dynamics

Dynamics mean how loudly or softly music should be played. There are various symbols to show different dynamics in music:

The Italian word *forte* or ***f*** means play loudly.

The Italian word *piano* or ***p*** means play softly.

The Italian word *fortissimo* or ***ff*** means play very loudly.

The Italian word *pianissimo* or ***pp*** means play very softly.

Put your clef before this music and decide which parts should be ***p***, ***pp***, ***f*** or ***ff***. Write in your dynamics under the notes, then play it.

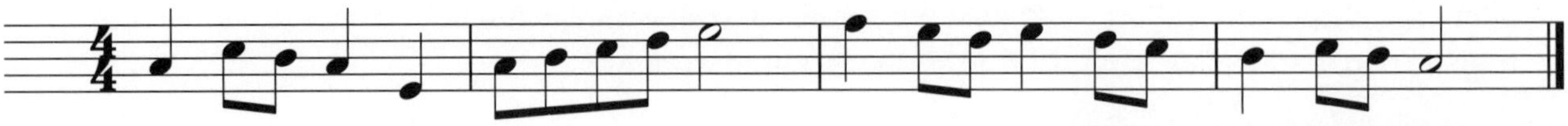

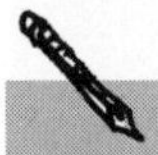

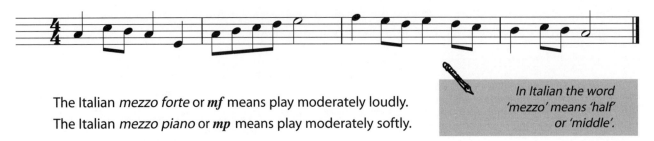

The Italian *mezzo forte* or ***mf*** means play moderately loudly.

The Italian *mezzo piano* or ***mp*** means play moderately softly.

In Italian the word 'mezzo' means 'half' or 'middle'.

Now we know the full range of dynamics we can put them in order from softest to loudest. Fill in the missing dynamics:

(53)

pp	***p***		***mf***		***ff***

The word *crescendo* or *cresc.* indicates that the music should get gradually louder. Sometimes this sign is used instead: <

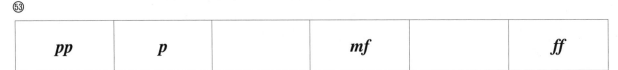

The words *diminuendo* (*dim.*) and *decrescendo* (*decresc.*) indicate that the music should get gradually softer. What sign do you think is used to show this? Draw it here:

Try to find the following dynamics in some of your own pieces:

mp in ____________________

cresc. or < in ____________________

pp in ____________________

dim. in ____________________

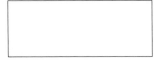

Articulation

Articulation tells us **how** to play the notes:

Staccato notes like this are played short and detached:

Legato notes like this are joined by a line called a slur and should be played smoothly:

Remember that articulation does not affect the rhythm – so you still have to count.

Put your clef before this extract, then play or sing it observing the articulation:

Add your own clef and join notes of the same pitch with a tie. Then draw slurs and staccato signs where you think they would work best and sing or play it on your instrument:

Changing tempo

If we want music to get gradually slower we use the word *ritardando* or *rit.* or sometimes *rallentando* or *rall.*

If we want music to get gradually faster we use the word *accelerando* or *accel.*

Put your clef at the start of this extract and play it through. Decide where you want it to get slower and/or faster. Write in the correct words above the stave to show this.

Then add in some articulation and dynamics to this extract, and play the final version through.

Italian terms

Musical notation began in Italy so we traditionally use Italian words. We have already learnt some in signs and symbols, dynamics, articulation and changing tempo.

At the start of a piece of music you will usually see a word or words to indicate the tempo (speed). Sometimes it also indicates mood or style of the music. Some of the most common ones are given below. Look through the music you are playing at the moment and see if you can find any of them:

Italian	English	Name of the piece
Vivace	Very fast	
Allegro	Fast and lively	
Andante	At a walking pace	
Largo	Slow	
Adagio	Very slow	
Grave	Extremely slowly	

Here are some additional instructions. Again, fill in the box if you can find any of the following terms in your music:

Italian	English	Name of the piece
più	more	
poco	little	
molto	very	
meno	less	
mosso	speed or pace	
da capo	repeat from the beginning	
dal segno	repeat from the sign 𝄋	
Fine	the end	

Now let's put some of these Italian words together. Write down the meaning of the following words. At the end write down any other Italian terms you come across in your pieces, and ask your teacher what they mean.

Italian	English	Name of the piece
più f		
meno mosso		
staccatissimo		
poco rall.		
molto accel.		
da capo al fine		
dal segno al fine		